BEFORE AND AFTER
THE DARKNESS

Also by Susan Noble

Collected Poems

The Dream of Stairs: A Poem Cycle

Drifting Between Empty Tramlines

A Flock of Blackbirds

Inside the Stretch of My Heart

BEFORE AND AFTER THE DARKNESS

Selected Poems

Susan Noble

AESOP Poets
Oxford

AESOP Poets
An imprint of AESOP Publications
Martin Noble Editorial / AESOP
28 Abberbury Road, Oxford OX4 4ES, UK
www.aesopbooks.com

First paperback edition published by AESOP Publications
Copyright (c) 2014 The Estate of Susan Noble

ISBN: 978-1-910301-13-5

Contents

Preface		vii
Publisher's note		xi
1	*Winter Dampness*	17
2	*Reality Smiles*	18
3	*Whale Ideas*	19
4	*The Past*	21
5	*Through the Needle's Eye*	22
6	*Honesty*	23
7	*Something Is Lost*	24
8	*Luck*	25
9	*Saturday Night*	26
10	*Frightened of the Night*	27
11	*Dreams Talk*	28
12	*Blue*	29
13	*Double Edged*	30
14	*Fall*	31
15	*Topsy-Turvy*	32
16	*Two o'clock*	33
17	*Cracked Heart*	34
18	*Geometry of the Mind*	35
19	*The Consolation of Illusion*	36
20	*Will*	37
21	*Between Before and After*	38
22	*The Hum of Silence*	39
23	*Guilt*	40
24	*Combat*	41
25	*Infatuation*	42
26	*Black and White Universe*	43
27	*Cynic*	44

CONTENTS

28	*Kite*	45
29	*Primary School*	46
30	*Adulthood*	47
31	*Three Witches*	48
32	*Shades*	49
33	*Deserted*	50
34	*Salt*	52
35	*Before and After the Darkness*	54
36	*Future Nightmare*	55
37	*Earthquake*	56
38	*Not to See Him Again*	58
39	*Whale*	59
40	*Ants*	60
41	*The Squatter*	61
42	*Housewarming*	62
43	*Rhythm*	63
44	*It Will Pass*	64
45	*Lunch*	65
46	*Memories of a Solemn Childhood*	66
47	*Beethoven*	67
48	*Day and Night*	68
49	*Fire Song*	69
50	*Time Frozen*	70
51	*Time's Whispering Silence*	71
52	*Crocodile*	72
53	*Silver*	74
54	*Fear of the Lone Self*	75
55	*Tree and Leaf*	77
Index of Poems		79
Index of First Lines		87

Preface

About the book

Before and After the Darkness is the companion volume to the collections *Inside the Stretch of the Heart* and *The Dream of Stairs: A Poem Cycle*. The last of these was privately printed as a posthumous memorial volume in 1975, a year after my sister Susan Noble's untimely death in 1974 at the age of 31.

Susan wrote the poems in batches of half a dozen or more, from 1965 onwards, in what she described as manic bursts of creativity, announcing with her typically light-hearted ironic self-depreciation, 'The muse has struck me!' But these poems are anything but light-hearted, and even a first reading will reveal clearly that levity is not on the menu in a universe 'Where there are no jokes / And people do not pretend.'

Susan's output in the final ten years of her life was prolific and to mark the fortieth anniversary of her death, the poems in this present collection have been published for the first time, together with a revised, expanded edition of *The Dream of Stairs*.

Three other volumes are being simultaneously published: *Collected Poems*, incorporating the above three poetry collections in one volume; and two prose works: *A Flock of Blackbirds*, featuring a selection of Susan's short stories and novellas, and her novel *Drifting Between Empty Tramlines*.

Many of the poems in *Before and After the Darkness* and *Inside the Stretch of My Heart* are triggered by the quotidian experience of living and working in central London in the late 1960s and early 1970s, yet beneath the fragile surface of her acute observations of domestic and office life in the city, intensely spiritual insights are being played out, sometimes delicately, sometimes shockingly, but always movingly.

Profits from the sales of all six volumes are being donated to three charities: Mind, the Samaritans and Sane. For more details, see page ix. Facsimiles of the original typescripts and manuscripts are available online at:

www.aesopbooks.com/susannoble

Martin Noble
Oxford, 2014

About the author

Brought up in South London, my sister, Susan Noble, was the second of three children. Her childhood was enriched by being part of our large and closely-knit Jewish family. Unfortunately stricken by polio (then known as infantile paralysis) in her early years, Susan went through life with a degree of physical handicap which she was to overcome with courage and determination.

Educated at Croydon High School, Susan studied English at Somerville College, Oxford. After graduating, Susan worked in London, first at the Royal National Institute for the Blind, dictating books for transcription into Braille, and later at the National Central Library in London, where she qualified as a Chartered Librarian.

Susan's exceptional sensitivity was reflected in the prolific outpouring of poems that make up *Before and After the Darkness*, *Inside the Stretch of My Heart* and *The Dream of Stairs*. In these intense, haunting poems, she chronicles her personal response to the world around her, while vividly portraying the inner landscape of her mental and emotional struggle.

Judith Frankel
Netanya, 2014

Susan Noble

One's first impression of Susan was of fragility. She was an acutely sensitive person, but her physical and emotional fragility really masked a very great spiritual strength.

Her sensitivity indeed was not directed only towards herself, but towards others. She was sensitive to the needs of others, and her strength and also perhaps some of her inner conflicts came from a deep desire for goodness which could not be matched in reality by the world as she found it.

Susan passionately wished to be independent; she struggled for it from the time she went to university, and throughout her work as a librarian, and she was able to maintain it to the very end.

There was an intellectual and emotional intensity which burned within her and which predominantly found outward expression in her writing and when she expressed herself thus she did so with great imaginative power and also with an uncompromising honesty and integrity.

The late Rabbi Dr David Goldstein
South London, July 1974

Publisher's note

All profits from the sale of this volume
are being donated to the following charities:

The National Association for Mental Health
www.mind.org.uk

SAMARITANS

www.samaritans.org

SANE

www.sane.org.uk

Before and After the Darkness

There at the centre
All other objects dropped
Now
Frozen
Into a realisation of what has been lost
The curves and angles shudder
Between before and after
Swing into focus.

from *Between Before and After*

If I could help you along the way, my love
I would do so willingly
But there is too much work to be done
For one person or even two or three
Too much darkness to be swept away
Darkness and shadows
Equivocal and obscure.

from *Before and After the Darkness*

This world is topsy-turvy
There is no cause for blame.

from *Topsy Turvy*

1   *Winter Dampness*

Winter dampness is a fungus
Time to rehearse one's shortcomings
The metallic sky rings guilt
Toast and oranges by the kitchen stove
Are an artifice
To hide the shivering afternoon
Out of doors the pavement clinks into bruises
The double glazing of the shopping parade
Is numb with furniture and lampshades
Comforts that are cleared away
By the blind silver light

2   *Reality Smiles*

Reality smiles,
Does not grow any happier
Though it repeats the pattern daily.
Two facing mirrors reflect forever
Into a tunnel of glass arches
Clear as cold liquid
Seeking
I find sometimes a new place
Invisible
Rippled.

3   *Whale Ideas*

Whale ideas
Blubber home
We press on
Further to find
New reflections
In the lashes of mud-water
That sink into us
We are fish
And fish blubber
And see island
And dry land is not sea
A long way ahead
Filters
Flesh through the network
One day
We will look at the rising sun
Gold sparks above the sea
Nearly forgotten
Now pierced
By the surprised eye
Which sees
The heat against the liquid

Gold as memory
Flesh the light of the sun like oil
On the curious wetness
Of penetrated water.

4   *The Past*

Canniballed
Not aware
I have absorbed them
Into my first
They multiply
Like worms
That make the calm good
Tell old stars in eyes
That grew angels
Every one of them
I will keep
Revolving
Will not let dissolve
The memory
Never throw back
To an old happening

5 *Through the Needle's Eye*

In me
You stay
White fire
Along the day
Spindle the thread
Through the needle's eye
Point flashes cold and then hot
Through the peach of the skin
Always I see the dark
A sky, growing old
And eyes
Seeing

6   *Honesty*

Strength of you
Crag of shoulders
Wedge of eyes
Scrutinise
Straight as the crow flies
Truthful
Where the silhouettes around you
Sharpen in surprise
And the window cuts the sky
Into fire

7   *Something Is Lost*

Crack
Between dawn and morning
The curtains half shut onto a grey sky
Something is lost, broken
In the hanging air.
The stove is grimed with rings of food
Crisped against the enamel
Pounding in my head
The face of a man
Resentful
Stirs out of my grasp
Lurches away
The carpet has knobs on
The clock ticks.

8 Luck

A gratuitous gift
A letter of good fortune flutters to the mat
I read it uneasily
Strange twist of normal combat to win
The bubble in my head swelling to a globe
And thoughts drift unconnected in the vacuum
Cannot enjoy the winning
The success
Separates me from living.

9 *Saturday Night*

Saturday night
The broken down fire
Fuses the flat
Into an older winter
Red flares across the snow
As the moon treads heavily
Soon the wolves will sing and howl
The curves of ice will sweep across the earth
The hulk of sky and mountaintops
Will spin in sleep
No-one cares
Alone
The sleeping bodies
Wait
For the whine to abate
And roast back into black comfort
Breathing like metronomes
To balance
The terror
Out there

10   *Frightened of the Night*

I am frightened of the night
That suckers the room
Into a standing pool
Where cars scream in the distance
A shaft of light blows an oblong ghost
Onto the painting on the wall
Around the bed
Hang old misdeeds
Pincered like crabs
That will punish me
I am frightened of the night
That suckers the room
Into a standing pool

11   *Dreams Talk*

She slept in a chair by the table
At her side of the room
While we talked with the windows open
And the wind rolled over her hair
It ruffled the black strands into clouds over her neck
And our talking crept into her dreams
Her peacefulness spread over us
It soothed us into silence
And her dreams began to talk out loud
And she spoke our conversation
The voice of her past life
The child that she had been spoke out
And spoke to the children in us
Rolling us back into her past
The open window ruffled
The waves of air, the dust on the floor
And past and present crashed
Into a drama of sleep.

12 *Blue*

Thinking is away from the grain
Of blue indolence
Needlepoints that flash hotly
Into staccato
The old man in the watch-shop
Has meshed
Amongst the pink chrome
Slowly totters up the bill
Alarm bells ring
Soon the blue sky will descend.

13   *Double Edged*

Love, once wanted,
Panacea to blunt all edges
And turn the pavements pink
Is not so
It is a knife into the heart
Where black and gold
Crack into shattering explosion
Frightens the eye away.

If I had loved one jot less
There would have been no self-murder
In this giving
If he had loved one jot less
There would have been no destruction
In my surrender.

14 *Fall*

Blighted
Earth waved return to its former crystal,
Eden blue and red and green,
Washed colours in the rain;
Feels the eagle
Hover over its cracks,
Split
Into trembling.
The wing-shafts whirr and hover;
Brain engulfment.

15 *Topsy-Turvy*

The criminal is ill,
Steals in surprise.
Stick arms in hospitals
Wait for sympathy
White as grapes
This world is topsy-turvy
There is no cause for blame.

16   *Two o'clock*

Net curtains quiver
Like loops of jelly
The gable opposite
Presses over windows
Peacock blue
Whistle and moan of traffic
Damp air floating to dispersal
This two o'clock is too peaceful
To be real

17 *Cracked Heart*

Heart cracked into jagged edges
Like a knife through paper
Leaves the spikes
To prick into consciousness
For the rest of this life
There is no mending;
The black blood has gushed out
Filtered from the red,
That bubbles into rebirth.

18   *Geometry of the Mind*

His eyes
Black
Will hypnotise
Force my mind
To bend a right-angle to his own.
The will
Will never submit
To this geometry
Black eyes
Upon my black fear
Can force a rape.

19   *The Consolation of Illusion*

The consolation of illusion
Love and light
To clean with over-exposure
The grimy patches
A fixative would do better the trick
To see
Black upon grey upon white
The cold knife edge
Saw amputating limb
The cut of day

20 *Will*

The will frittered out
Would not obey
Turned perverse
I tried to call it back
They tried to call it back
It ran screaming over the earth in all directions
The coal beneath the clumpy tree trunks
Turned black
Filamented into spider roots
We waited
A stone's throw
A flicker of wind
That scratched and teased the hush
In expectation
And swivelled
To the right key
Pleased to turn back.
Back into turning

21   *Between Before and After*

Falling short
Compromise
As the air filters into yellow and blue
From what was conceived
To what has grown to be
This instant
Flickering dust
And choice of words
Could be perfected
To a pearl
Static
There at the centre
All other objects dropped
Now
Frozen
Into a realisation of what has been lost
The curves and angles shudder
Between before and after
Swing into focus.

22 *The Hum of Silence*

Hot silence
Divides the air
Into good and evil
Listen to the hum of the world
Blink
Numbly.
Now if a curtain of moon
Would eclipse the sun
And turn the world into a black grimace
Where would we laugh
Which part of the cheek would grin,
Dissolved with the palsy
Of light
Blank gold of light
Releases the terror
Throw off daytime shapes
A kaleidoscope
To divert the heart from a love
That can never be released
Never swell into a burnt flood
Trapped inside the hum of silence
Of the revolving earth.

23 *Guilt*

Gilted leaves
That paint the sun
Over their web of spider-stem
The guilt I feel
For past misdeeds
That cannot be
In knotted pain
The crab that grew
When he told me
Of the guilt I own
This clod of earth
Twists into folds
Beneath the sun
The evening light
Goes down
Goes down
One day will roll away
Beyond
The edge of some world basket home
The retribution will begin
The guilt I own
The knotted crab
Will tell its gold.

24   *Combat*

If you could love the person
Whom you most dislike in all the world
Then you would have conquered fear
To kiss the repulsive lips
And smile with feeling warmth
Upon the face you loathe.
If you could spend one day and night
In the house which you most abhor
Then you would have conquered your fear.
But here is no victory possible,
Only an endless sidetrack along a devious maze
Away from the dragons that people
The kaleidoscope of your mind.

25 *Infatuation*

Every time I fall in love
Sharpness of sunlight, silhouette
And glow of silver reflection
The stab of passing you in the street
All faces grow alike, reflect the same expression
And I am thrown into the magnetic pool
Of one personality
Then slowly the surface thickens,
The sharpness turns to wool
And there is only a cold gust of wind
Until the next figure
Walks clearly onto the scene.

26   *Black and White Universe*

One man was there
I loved
Face black and white
I cannot forget
Stays there in the centre
A reminder of the one
We cling to
Which way to go
Right or left
Or to stay there in the middle like a rock
Everyone
Has one man there in the centre
Black and white
To clock in on time
And watch the whim
Of the black and white universe.

27 Cynic

She speaks glibly of intellectual despair
And I see blackness in her eyes, her hair
Her smile cracks her face in two
And my peace of mind is blown over
From its upturned wave
And crumbled into drops of disbelief
Her laugh is grating
A macabre mockery
And echoes in my mind at midnight
Turning my eyes and hair black
In the hanging gloom.

28 *Kite*

I can never know you completely
The more I know the more I want
Can never reach the peak
Looped kite flying against the cream sky
Can never reach so high, high
If I could fly
And loop the loop to cling to the top
I would pull you down
Crash into the seeking grass below
Wet from the rain
Splash into the mud
I can never know you at all
Not at all
Just the tug of the breeze that lifts
A flicker here and there
And then slithers away
Into stillness.

29 *Primary School*

On a windy morning in October
The first week at school
Two rows of children were lining up
Hopping up and down
Pale legs turned orange in the damp air
In the school playground
A girl named Mary
A boy called Graham
Strange to meet other people in the wind
Each with different features
Fitting together like the faces we crayoned
That morning in the long gone schoolroom.

30   *Adulthood*

Hideous jollity
Kipper on the table
And a smear of margarine
Loudspeaker turned up full blast
Into words and noise and words
Battering ram of information
To churn through the kitchen sink water
That flows from an open tap
Onto the square handle
Of an upturned yellow beaker
The three walls press inwards leading me
Through the open doorway
And crack open the front door
To squeak through the bulge of the narrow hall
White stinging sky
Clap-shock of rebirth
Into a non-plastic world of rainwater
Soft moisture in the air
And the angry grey December
Stretching endlessly
Towards the city.

31   *Three Witches*

When my anger broods and stirs
Within me, black bubble liquid in a cauldron
And the three witches grin and leer
Over me, yellow teeth rotting in mirth
Hatred sizzles my love for you into distrust
And fear turns ice cold white skin trembling
As I wait for your retreating figure
To return and smile
But it remains far distant
And jealousy burns into my stomach
With wild insistence
The black bubbles brood
And the night sky outside
Hangs like a slate
Flat against the glass of the window
Pain against pane
Until gradually the old love rolls over me like a wave
And all I see are your shining eyes
And outstretched hands.

32 *Shades*

I see you shadow-bound
Between the circle of life and death
Grasping at every moment
An extra person to acknowledge your existence
I see you at the leaf-time
Brown evening shadows against the wall
When you are beige
A biscuit figure
Grinning and seizing the faces there
With a smile and a nod of the head
I know that to be dead
Is to be remembered
Yet I cannot act as you would wish
Hand outstretched, giving to all
In the face of every attack from the shades of night
For to me the night has no shades
And I have no need of these people.

33 *Deserted*

So many things given
Mornings that sweep open the sky
To set me free
And fluorescent twilights
Navy pools of night
Even the still band of ice
Across midday
That freezes the clamour into peace
So many things given
Then why should I mind
That you will not give
One word
One shadow of your presence?

The blank space
Through which furniture and walls protrude
In your place
Screams endlessly
A nightmare;
A vacuum;
A desert
Of being deserted.
One whiny woman
Cannot bring back all those who have escaped

Slipped through the tracks
To sweep open the sky alone
And break the navy pools of night
In solitude to regain
The still band of ice
For which they crave.

So many things
God has given me
In every place there are signs of Him
Then why do I see
Only the empty spaces
And no freedom?

34 *Salt*

Sunday afternoon,
White as salt
I walked over the dregs of the building site
In slow motion
A woman nearby pale with a broken arm
Placed each foot
Two inches in front of the other
And groaned with effort,
Swallowing two aspirins
The concrete blocks on either side
Washed clean the past
In slow waves of walking
Our cold eyes stared
Grey pupils, molasses of concrete
And as she passed over the bridge
I recognised the swing of navy skirt
And saw again the young smile
And hand outstretched with chalk
In the classroom of the fourth form
Through the windows the June sunshine
Streamed onto the walls
Of the chemistry block outside

And I knew that the past
Had been wiped clean as a slate
As clean as bromide paper
Left in the sun too long
And bleached from over-exposure
White as salt.

35   *Before and After the Darkness*

Things are not so easy for you now, my love
There is much work to be done
Much darkness to be swept away
As I walk along the bleak street I see
A Christmas tree
Red balls of light on khaki branches
The only Christmas tree I could give you
Would be a heap of lollipops for your children
For the child that you once were
Before the darkness came upon you
Before you saw too deeply within
If I could help you along the way, my love
I would do so willingly
But there is too much work to be done
For one person or even two or three
Too much darkness to be swept away
Darkness and shadows
Equivocal and obscure.

36   *Future Nightmare*

I dreamt I had a tiny ear growing inside my ear
And stood in the brown rustlight in a field of wheat
Yellow and buff leaves flopping crisp
Yet unwholesome
The cardboard cracks torn down
Between the possible and the unearthly
I had become a painted cartoon
On a packet of shredded wheat
And lived in a future era
When all things could grow awry,
In the barley and the rye
Dinosaurs wriggling along the fields
With grey charcoal hippos
Hanging vertical in the painted air.

37 *Earthquake*

The girl sways her pregnant hips
As she plays on the guitar
Silver rings, flash of light, sparks in the fire grate.
Slither through the silver grid
She sings a losing song
The song of those who have wasted hours
Washing, knitting, furlongs of wool
Who have slipped through the tracks in boredom
And hours of friendship snapped in two
By a letter gone astray
Dropped in the sizzling heat
At the end of a long day
The losers of this world
Gather together their energy
And form rings around her guitar strings
But no rings on her stubby fingers
No colour on her scrubbed white face
Chin jutting out squarely beneath ashen hair
And eyes like long blue fish
That slither and smile
As the audience around her swells pregnant
With all the ticking hours of her life

That have never been channelled into
Certitudes or bonds
Who have fallen away, disappeared
For men who have slipped away
Through the tracks in boredom
And only appear from time to time
Silver cools in the earthquakes of her songs
But smoulder under the ground
Between the cracks.

38   *Not to See Him Again*

Not to see him again
Never the eyes crinkling
Lips twisted
Into a smile
Not to speak to him again
No more answers
To insoluble questions
No more clues to a magical formula
For living
Not to laugh with him again
No eyebrows raised
With new apologies
Communicating where further communion
Was prevented
Now we are joined by the black ligaments
Of memory
Blood beats around the sinews
And can never rest
Lives on forever
In the hearth-fires
Of a generous heart

39 *Whale*

Despair, the whale
Swallows up the whole man
And then spews him out
To taste the golden waters
Beneath the dazzled sky.

40 *Ants*

Ideas
Like ants
Multiply, swarm and flock together
I am careful
Which way I turn
So as not to crush
A few thousand.

41   *The Squatter*

Bare carpet peeling off
Soft fluff
And on the walls a picture
Of the Maharaji
Gaudy colour posters
And unswept dust.
The squatter's clothes in a bundle
In front of the paint-smeared bat window
Which dazzles the naked room
Like a scream
After childbirth.

42 *Housewarming*

They scrub the drawers
And sweep clean the carpet of dust
Three unopened cases and two bags of provisions
Gradually
The room unfolds its colours
Like a tulip bending over its reflection
Until petal and water kiss
In one bubble of colour.
Outside
The May streets
Sways with birds and trees
Welcoming them
To their new home.

43 *Rhythm*

Each day month week
We polish shoes shine
Feathers dusted
Oven scrubbed
Face washed
In the blood of diurnal rhythm
Breakfasted many times
Car restarting on the same journey
Alarm-clock shrieking
Trapped in the twenty-four-hour
Game of chance
Again
Again
And again.

44 *It Will Pass*

May
Peace   birds   trees   sway
Welcome
Window looks onto rooftops
Pale cloud sky
Two youths saunter
Towards each other

Always
The past is made concise
Tied down to daylight frame
While the present
Muddles though
Blurred-edged

Every time
I feel suicidal
I remember this:
'It will pass' –
It helps me

45 *Lunch*

Four girls
Sharing gossip
At lunchtime
Hair tossing aside
In different shades of brown
One strand over this forehead
Two strands over that
Stab a tomato and pull this man
To pieces
Spear a lettuce-leaf and murder that one
Now a laugh
One joke
Two jokes
Three smiles
Four empty plates.
Silence.

46 *Memories of a Solemn Childhood*

Crisp voice, newly ironed
Along with the frilly white blouse,
Skirt swinging, flick back the hair
And run down the hall on pattering shoes.
Carnation scent, a belt of leather studded with gems,
Staccato laugh, pinching the world
Into delicate shapes of comedy,
Like an expert *patisseur*,
To slice reality into thin strips,
More manageable.
Gravity annihilated
By microscopic analysis,
Probing the components. seeking out the absurd.
Occasionally
To sink into a chair and cry,
Shoulders heaving,
Memories of a solemn childhood.

47 *Beethoven*

You teach me how to plumb the depths of pain
In tuneful melancholy probing deep.
Then numb my thoughts to quietness and peace
Inducing an unexpected, timeless sleep.

Your melodies each plead with me to listen
To their twofold message splaying from one source.

In artful harmony, which once perfected
Leaves nothing unresolved by its polished force.

48 *Day and Night*

The day slips across the murmuring sea of life
Borne aloft on a single wave, precarious and about to totter.
Despite the floating seaweed and driftwood that hinders
        its course
It travels from shore to shore with unrelenting regularity.
Never stopping to pause and survey the scenery
Or to give way to an oncoming intruder.
When a ship rumbles near at great force
And continues its journey in submarine silence
Until it reaches the far side,
When it is again restored to the breathing air.
Night comes on the face of the sea
And time glows with phosphorescent brightness
Illuminating the nocturnal world of fishes
Into a glowing unity.

49 *Fire Song*

I hung upon the splintering beam of oak
That shouldered me and pricked with cutting lashes,
But held me high above the burning timber
That crackled as it crumpled into ashes.

The flames subsided soon and turned to cinders
I swept them up and burnt my little finger.
It smarted but then drifted into numbness
And soon I overcame my hasty anger.

50 *Time Frozen*

Time frozen into ice-drops
Clings quietly to the branches
Of the pear tree by my window.
A gust of wind impels it into motion,
Scattering it into a myriad of pearls
That fall to the ground and clink bitterly
Regretting their release from immobility.
Once static, now reluctantly individual,
They drift sadly in all directions
Longing for the winter of eternity to chill them
Into icy permanence once more.

51 *Time's Whispering Silence*

I hear time's whispering silence in my ears,
A toneless beat that never stops to linger.
Sometimes it overtakes my drifting life
And leaves me far behind in useless anger.

I take a running leap to overtake it,
But trip upon the hurdles of existence
And when I try to grab its furtive sleeve
It slips away from me with slip persistence.

52 *Crocodile*

I know a man
Who goes to church every Sunday
And works in Moorgate in a black bowler hat,
Quite an ordinary man,
Except that when he was a boy
He read of the African jungle gleaming wild and free
And lived between lessons in a towering date-tree
Half a mile high
And whistled eerie songs to the crocodiles,
That squelched and chattered in the churning mud
Of the Lualaba River,
And stamped angrily on the crawling red ants
That used to invade his unobtrusive hide-out.

And when he was sixty and a half, he retired
And in return received a splendid watch of solid gold
To tick away his senile years of leisure,
When he was supposed to prune the rose-heads
And drink amiable cups of tea with his quiet, pleasant wife,

But instead he went straight to the zoo
And took home a tiny tame crocodile
With horny skin and tender eyes and flashing teeth
He fed it on raw meat and milk and peppermints,
Which crocodiles are supposed to greatly relish
And at last he was thoroughly absorbed,
Hauling up plates of food and whistling eerie songs.
Even his wife didn't seem to mind
In spite of all the squelching and spilt water
For she was quiet and pleasant.

53 *Silver*

Why, when I look at silver,
Can I not see the compound colour
White, grey and black
But see only the shiny metal surface?
And why, when I look at you and you and you
Can I not see the compound colours
But only the fixed image?

54 *Fear of the Lone Self*

This park greenery
Overwhelms
Like a memory of nausea
Damp tufts of grass upon clod of earth
Tickle the feet
With fear of the lone self.
The ruthless clock of time
Throbs noiselessly
Beneath the fertile veneer
Of the earth.
Hours spent in the naked light
Of the midnight room
And the opened book
Palling
After isolation
Waiting for the sound of the foot
Upon the stairs
The squeak of the rat

Now
Amidst running children
And sleeping torsos
Impossible to shout
'I am alone!'
Alone beneath a body of skin
Waiting
For what can never come to pass.

55   *Tree and Leaf*

Books   dust
Woolly paper   at edges
Torn covers   brittle spines
People reading, reading
All over the world
Swallowing indigestible phrases
As well as the old familiar
Concepts
Dust falls to
Floor
Outside trees grow to wood
To paper   to books
Hieroglyphics of black and white
Feeding the brain
Which feeds the body
Which moves among dust and wood and paper
And books and trees, where
The birds whistle happily
Having read nothing but the signs
Of tree and leaf

Index of Poems

Note: this index includes page numbers for poems published in the companion volumes, The *Dream of Stairs* and *Inside the Stretch of My Heart.*

* = this volume.
D = *The Dream of Stairs*
I = *Inside the Stretch of My Heart*

A

Acorn (I) 113

Acquiescence (I) 223

Adulthood* 47

After the Quarrel (D) 49

Afterwards (D) 184

Age (I) 103

Ago (D) 144

Aim, The (D) 65

Alien (D) 183

Anchor-man (D) 206

Ants* 60

Apple-Blossom Scent (D) 24

Ascetic, The (I) 229

Aversion (I) 31

Awakening (D) 171

B

Bag, The (D) 122

Ballad (D) 73

Ballroom, The (D) 38

Bank Holiday (I) 85

Beethoven * 67

Before and After the Darkness * 54

Being (D) 138

Belief (D) 204

Between Before and After* 38

Bio-Energetics (I) 140

Black and White Universe * 488

Black Star (D) 170

Blackbird (D) 98

Blind Man, The (I) 67

Blue* 29

Bluffer, The (I) 49

Boast, The (I) 59

Bones (I) 91

Bore, The (I) 70
Boredom (I) 95
Brain (I) 182
Bubble (I) 62
Bureaucrat, The (I) 34
Burnt Out by the Shadows (D) 63
Bus (I) 115

C

Cactus (I) 121
Call (I) 25
Camera (I) 232
Cave God (D) 208
Chain (I) 40
Change (D) 91
Chastity D 33
Chawton House (D) 181
Chicken Bone (D) 59
Choice, The (I) 186
Christmas Eve (I) 159
Clam (D) 58
Combat* 41
Communication in Silence (I) 41
Concrete Ground (D) 82
Confession (D) 47
Conflict (D) 165
Consolation of Illusion, The* 36
Continue (D) 141
Conviction (D) 137
Corn Song (D) 214
Couple, The (D) 45
Corrupt (D) 169

Cotton-Wool Words (D) 55
Cousins (D) 28
Cracked Heart* 34
Creation (D) 135
Crocodile* 72
Crossed Line (I) 46
Crowd (I) 65
Current of Belief (I) 198
Cut-outs D 53
Cycle (I) 240
Cynic* 44

D

Dance, The (D) 211
Day (I) 23
Day and Night * 68
Deaf Ear, The (I) 169
Decision (D) 151
Deserted* 50
Development (D) 148
Devils (D) 160
Disillusionment (D) 88
Display (I) 187
Distrust (I) 184
Divorce (I) 215
Double Biology (I) 109
Double Edged* 30
Double Glazing (I) 199
Doubt (D) 167
Downpour (I) 101
Dragons' Teeth (I) 80
Dream of Oxford (I) 158

Dream of Stairs, The (D) 76
Dreams Talk* 28
Duality (D) 75
Duel (D) 161
Dust (I) 42

E
Earthquake* 56
Egg (I) 179
Enemy, The (I) 75
Energy (D) 138
Ephraim (I) 105
Evening Class, The (I) 133
Evil (I) 195
Evolution (D) 205
Eyes (I) 206

F
Façade (I) 197
Facets (D) 64
Fainting, The (I) 154
Fall* 31
Fallen Away (I) 234
Falling (D) 39
False Image (D) 69
Fear (D) 136
Fear of the Lone Self* 75
Feathers (D) 120
Fifty Per Cent (I) 219
Filter (I) 181
Fire (I) 237

Fire Song * 69
First Love (D) 37
Fishes (I) 60
Fishing (I) 93
Flight (I) 125
Flock of Blackbirds, A (I) 79
Food-Time (I) 118
Foretaste (I) 137
Forwards (D) 191
Four-Leaved (I) 211
Friday Afternoons (I) 83
Frightened of the Night* 27
Frost (I) 224
Fulcrum (D) 106
Future, The (I) 194
Future Nightmare* 55

G
Geometry of the Mind* 35
Gift (D) 57
Giving (D) 94
God and Satan (I) 191
Gold Door (D) 193
Grape Picking (D) 34
Grief (D) 187
Growth (I) 100
Guilt* 40

H
Hard Road, The (D) 23
Heat (D) 114

81

Holocaust (D) 164
Honesty* 23
Hospital in Winter (D) 86
Housewarming* 62
Hum of Silence, The* 39
Hunger (I) 117
Hypnosis (I) 139

I

I Wonder What This Constellation Will Be (D) 190
Illusion (D) 124
Image (I) 132
Incommunicado (I) 52
Inconsolation (D) 197
Individuation (D) 156
Infatuation* 42
Infection (I) 221
Insect (I) 165
Insight (D) 200
Instant (I) 190
Intercom (I) 37
Interior (I) 143
Interruption (I) 84
Interval (D) 130
Involvement (I) 214
It Will Pass* 64

J

Jealousy (I) 183
Joke, The (I) 69
Journey (I) 24

K

Keyboard (D) 107
Kibbutz (I) 71
Killing, The (D) 46
Kite* 45
Knowledge (D) 209

L

Label (I) 129
Last Respects (I) 141
Laughter, The (D) 52
Launderette (I) 43
Lemon (I) 111
Leucotomy (D) 85
Life Story (D) 26
Line of Memory, The (I) 200
Living-Room (I) 57
Lizard (D) 119
Losing, The (D) 104
Loss (I) 150
Lost Between Stone Basins (I) 102
Lost (D) 79
Love (D) 134
Luck* 25
Lunch* 65
Lunchtime (I) 63

M

Madwoman, The (D) 95
Malaise (I) 106
Maternity (D) 146

Meditating (I) 225
Meditation (D) 74
Meeting (I) 92
Memories of a Solemn Childhood* 66
Memory (I) 178
Midday (D) 35
Midnight at the Station (I) 152
Misunderstanding (I) 88
Moment (I) 47
Monday Morning (I) 29
Moon-Treasure (D) 77
Morning Break (I) 44
Morning (I) 28
Mouse (I) 164
Museum Piece (I) 98

N
Nail Armour (D) 115
Nature (D) 143
Needlepoint (I) 210
Neurasthenia (D) 83
Nice Child (D) 27
Night (I) 149
Nightmare (D) 121
Nine to Five-Thirty (I) 33
Ningo Pin, The (D) 196
No Danger (I) 135
No Further Can I Go (I) 245
No Mother (D) 147
No Resting Place (I) 220
Nocturne (D) 125
Not to See Him Again* 58

O
Occupational Therapy (I) 231
Off Peak (I) 68
Old Woman (I) 110
On the Steps (I) 97
Onion (D) 93
Open Door, The (D) 123
Outsize (I) 74
Over-Exposure (I) 201
Oyster (I) 208

P
Panorama (D) 168
Paper Children (I) 39
Parasite (I) 108
Park-Time (I) 86
Parting (D) 50
Party Games (I) 156
Party Time (I) 155
Passing (D) 62
Passive Involvement (I) 168
Past, The* 21
Peace (I) 247
Percentage (D) 89
Photo (I) 218
Pier (I) 123
Pity (I) 90
Platform (I) 153
Poet, The (I) 172
Poetry (D) 126
Portent (I) 51
Praise (D) 219

Preserve (D) 202

Preview (D) 29

*Primary School** 46

Protection (D) 41

Psychology (I) 192

Pulse (D) 140

Puppet (D) 142

Q

Quarrel, The (D) 48

Question (D) 158

Questions and Answers (I) 188

Quick Birth (D) 25

R

Rainy Day in the Tourist Season (I) 87

Rat-Race (I) 203

Reading (I) 48

Reality (I) 160

*Reality Smiles** 18

Reclamation (D) 166

Reconciliation (D) 207

Reflector (I) 204

Regeneration (D) 101

Regret (D) 90

Rejection (D) 51

Release (D) 149

Remember (D) 70

Reminder (I) 167

Rendezvous, The (D) 36

Respect for the Elders (I) 227

Restoration (D) 68

Resurgence (D) 192

Return (D) 189

Revelation (D) 81

*Rhythm** 63

Roaming (I) 180

Rope (D) 66

Rosanna (I) 136

Roses (D) 187

Routine (I) 134

S

Sacrifice (I) 233

*Salt** 52

Sanity (I) 193

Sartoris (I) 36

Saturday Afternoon (I) 114

*Saturday Night** 26

Save This Soul (D) 195

Scapegoat's Cry, The (I) 185

Schizophrenia (D) 84

Search, The (I) 170

Security (D) 210

See-Saw (D) 105

Selfhood (D) 128

Separation (D) 56

*Shades** 49

Shadows (I) 89

She Searched for Happiness (D) 182

Shell (D) 133

Shock (D) 185

Shyness (I) 142

Signs (D) 203
Silence (D) 177
Silk-Worm (I) 99
Silver* 74
Sin (D) 80
Singer, The (D) 113
Six Haikus (I) 226
Six o'clock (I) 124
Skull-Light (D) 127
Smile (D) 44
Smile, The (I) 209
Smiled upon a Face (I) 239
Snowdrop (I) 228
Something Is Lost* 24
Song of a Schizophrenic Monk (D) 112
Song of the Crow (I) 235
Sophistication (I) 217
Soul, The (D) 198
Spellbound (D) 40
Spider (D) 129
Spiral of Light (D) 60
Spur (D) 163
Squatter, The* 61
Stepping Outside (I) 144
Stifled (I) 82
Stones, The (I) 126
Street Dance (I) 81
Success (I) 207
Suicide (D) 175
Summer (I) 61
Summer Evening (I) 130
Sun on the Track (I) 244
Surprise (I) 145

T

Talents, The (D) 150
Teatime (I) 96
Telephone (I) 45
Television (I) 166
Ten Days of Penitence (I) 177
Those Who Do Not Question Much (I) 104
Three Witches* 48
Through the Barrier (I) 38
Through the Needle's Eye* 22
Tightrope (I) 205
Time (I) 26
Time Frozen * 70
Time Machine (I) 94
Time Suspended (D) 108
Time's Whispering Silence * 71
To Create (D) 19
To Forestall (I) 112
To Grieve (D) 186
To Speak (D) 215
To Write (I) 173
Topsy-Turvy* 32
Torpor (I) 53
Trafalgar (I) 73
Tree and Leaf* 77
Trendy People (I) 138
Tryptich (D) 157
Tube (I) 131
Tube-Time (I) 32
Tulip (I) 238
Tunnel (D) 145
Turbulence (I) 196

Twentieth Century (D) 155
Twins (D) 162
Two Cures (I) 212
Two o'clock* 33
Two Sides (I) 213

U
Ugliness (I) 58
Ugly, The (D) 97

V
Vacuum (I) 72
Verdure (I) 107
View (I) 122
Vision (D) 103
Vision, The (D) 111

W
Waiter, The (I) 119
Waiting, The (D) 116
Waitress, The (I) 120
Wakening (D) 102
Waking (I) 27
Wallflower (I) 246
Wandering Through the Days (D) 61
War Baby (I) 230
Wasted Years (I) 222
Water (D) 172
Water-Bird (D) 54
Waves (D) 199

We Follow Our Gods (I) 236
Wedding, The (D) 67
Weep Before God (D) 174
Whale* 59
Whale Ideas* 19
When His Arms Closed Around You (D) 43
When Morning Is Whiter than Shell (I) 30
When the Door Opens (D) 194
When the Hands Freeze Cold, (D) 78
When You Love Someone So Strangely (D) 42
Why Write? (I) 171
Widow Spider (I) 216
Will* 37
Will, The (I) 189
Winter (I) 151
Winter Dampness* 17
Worms (I) 50
Writing (I) 174

Y
Yellow Flame (D) 212
Yoga (I) 163
Yoga Dance (D) 110

Index of First Lines

Note: this index includes page numbers for poems published in the companion volumes, The *Dream of Stairs* and *Inside the Stretch of My Heart.*

* = this volume.

D = *The Dream of Stairs*

I = *Inside the Stretch of My Heart*

Line	Poem	Book	Page

A

A flock of blackbirds / They cry and cry	*A Flock of Blackbirds*	I	79
A frightening thing is memory	*Memory*	I	178
A glass of water and a tube of	*Suicide*	D	175
A gratuitous gift / A letter of good fortune	*Luck*	*	25
A guilt I feel, which is not needed, yet	*The Scapegoat's Cry*	I	185
A hidden chunk / Vulnerable / When	*Reality*	I	160
A jade silk-worm in the gallery	*Silk-Worm*	I	99
A man and a woman in a restaurant	*The Joke*	I	69
A phone-call from a woman / Who was	*Two Sides*	I	213
A poem cannot be contrived wilfully	*To Create*	D	19
A ring of friends, arms linked softly	*The Dance*	D	211
A shy polythene bag / Keeps the washing	*Shyness*	I	142
A swarm of birds fly fanlike overhead	*Panorama*	D	168
A tightrope of people / Every word must	*Tightrope*	I	205
A typewriter tapping, dust upon my desk	*Morning Break*	I	44
A wide expanse of gleaming spirals	*The Dream of Stairs*	D	76

After a long gap between poem / And poem	*Writing*	I	174
After all this time / Only a brick wall left	*Divorce*	I	215
After the broad road, / White as a pillar	*Dragons' Teeth*	I	80
After the cinema / The painted eyes and	*Christmas Eve*	I	159
After the quarrel / We sat in the night-	*After the Quarrel*	D	49
After the visitors departed / Slowly from	*Yoga*	I	163
All digging down to the same roots	*Meditating*	I	225
All that summer / The trees cracked	*First Love*	D	37
An all-devouring void inside me bleats	*Hunger*	I	117
Anchor-man, / Black as the night you are	*Anchor-man*	D	206
Apple-blossom scent, / Sickly strong	*Apple-Blossom Scent*	D	24
At certain times of the day / The time of	*The Stones*	I	126
At one o'clock, / Head swollen to a	*Bubble*	I	62
At the back of the moon, / Beyond the	*Moon-Treasure*	D	77
At the bottom of my mind's cave	*Cave God*	D	208
At the end of the long day / When the	*Remember*	D	70
At this moment, / I have curved round	*Moment*	I	47
At three o'clock / The line that cuts the	*Roses*	D	187

B

Baby breathing, mother peeping	*Development*	D	148
Bank holiday Monday white afternoon	*Interruption*	I	84
Bare carpet peeling off / Soft fluff	*The Squatter*	*	61
Beyond the footlights of the open-air	*Summer Evening*	I	130
Birds singing silver / Outside rain-	*Sartoris*	I	36
Black star / Make me strong / Against	*Black Star*	D	170
Blighted / Earth waved return to its	*Fall*	*	31
Blue aproned lady waddles to and fro	*Teatime*	I	96
Blue cushions / Plumped out	*Living-Room*	I	57
Books dust / Woolly paper at edges	*Tree and Leaf*	*	77
Bonds that break and merge / Day in	*Chain*	I	40
Born to a bellow of music outside the	*Life Story*	D	26

| Bought on an impulse, / It cost three days | *The Bag* | D | 122 |
| Brown and pink arms / And faces | *Crowd* | I | 65 |

C

Can it ever be recovered, / Integrity of	*Restoration*	D	68
Can never give enough, / As much as I	*Giving*	D	94
Can you not accept the fact / That I can	*Fifty Per Cent*	I	219
Canniballed / Not aware	*The Past*	*	21
Cannot feel a proper sorrow, / Cannot	*To Grieve*	D	186
Cannot find peace of mind, / Blue sky	*Turbulence*	I	196
Cannot live glad hours all the time	*The Open Door*	D	123
Cannot trust you, / Though know you well	*Distrust*	I	184
Cats spawn kittens. / Sun ties cellophane	*Growth*	I	100
Changed. / The white skin was still the	*Meeting*	I	92
Charcoal drawings / Fading into fibres	*Museum Piece*	I	98
Circle / Shoes in the morning	*The Bureaucrat*	I	34
Cold clatter of feet against the pavement	*Concrete Ground*	D	82
Cold feet on an office afternoon	*Boredom*	I	95
Cotton-wool words, / Cloud-spun	*Cotton-Wool Words*	D	55
Cousins / Are siblings once removed	*Cousins*	D	28
Crack / Between dawn and morning	*Something Is Lost*	*	24
Cricklewood in dust, / Garbage gleaming	*Saturday Afternoon*	I	114
Crisp voice, newly ironed / Along with	*Memories of a Solemn*	*	66
Crossing the road / I though I recognised	*False Image*	D	69
Curiosity infinite / There is much work	*Yellow Flame*	D	212
Curiously / Relieved I stare at the knife	*Six o'clock*	I	124
Cut out with regret, / Pull back into	*Regret*	D	90

D

| Daily routine of / Coil upon coil of | *Nine to Five-Thirty* | I | 33 |
| Despair, the whale / Swallow up the | *Whale* | * | 59 |

89

Discovered / Sucking slowly on a straw *Midday* D 35
Do not be dependent upon the one *Sacrifice* I 233
Down sticks of rain, / Neck gasping fish *Downpour* I 101

E

Each day month week / We polish shoes *Rhythm* * 63
Each one of us / Will one day be broken *Forwards* D 191
Endless book of days / Each night *Journey* I 24
Ephraim in his bedsitter / Smooths out *Ephraim* I 105
Every day / Springs forth twins *Energy* D 138
Every time I fall in love / Sharpness of *Infatuation* * 42
Everyone must bear between their fingers *When the Hands...* D 78

F

Fallen away / From the old God-love- *Being* D 138
Falling short / Compromise / As the air *Between Before and* * 38
Fear of motherhood. / A broken glass *No Mother* D 147
Five different faculties have we unknowing *Eyes* I 206
Fixed / Upon a tulip / I saw / Blue tinged *Tulip* I 238
Flames and torture-rack of a Tudor epic *Stepping Outside* I 144
Fools / That grin and have faith *Those Who Do Not* I 104
For four years we have worked in the *Communication in* I 41
Force open these eyelids shuttered so *Waking* I 27
Four girls / Sharing gossip / At lunchtime *Lunch* * 65
Frost and fog through the windows *View* I 122
Frozen fingernails turning yellow *Blackbird* D 98

G

Gilted leaves / That paint the sun *Guilt* * 40
God / Spreads his / Warmth and peace *Praise* D 219

Grey slaps that peel down / To neat shapes *Occupational Therapy* I   231

H

Hair aflame with the heat, / Eyes	*The Reading*	I	48
Hatred dwells among people, / Like	*Verdure*	I	107
He mocked her drawing, / Black criss-	*The Killing*	D	46
Heart cracked into jagged edges / Like	*Cracked Heart*	*	34
Heat dissolves me, frees the barriers	*Heat*	D	114
Her head is cider-swollen to a bubble	*No Danger*	I	135
Her voice hit the air with a subtle sweep	*The Singer*	D	113
Hidden in a telephone kiosk / On an	*Last Respects*	I	141
Hideous jollity / Kipper on the table and	*Adulthood*	*	47
High above the earth / Upon a tightrope	*Rope*	D	66
His anger murdered her with eagle eyes	*Bones*	I	91
His eyes / Black / Will hypnotise	*Geometry of the M.*	*	35
His moccasins spattered with green mud	*The Rendezvous*	D	36
His poised / Eyes, / Leaping fish	*Fishing*	I	93
His writing is more real to him than life.	*To Write*	I	173
Hot silence / Divides the air / Into good	*The Hum of Silence*	*	39
Hypocritical / With each change of	*Involvement*	I	214

I

I accept this, the stifled past / I can endure	*Acquiescence*	I	223
I am a child of the twentieth century	*Twentieth Century*	D	155
I am a puppet, / Jerking one and two and	*Puppet*	D	142
I am a shell / Catching echoes of the past	*Shell*	D	133
I am a turnip gone mouldy / And my top	*Corrupt*	D	169
I am an egg. / A black band in the middle	*Egg*	I	179
I am frightened of the night / That suckers	*Frightened of the N.*	*	27
I am one person / Sometimes the snowdrop	*Snowdrop*	I	228
I am pale and white / Calm and quiet	*Chastity*	D	33

I can never know you completely	*Kite*	*	45
I could tear you out of me,	*Chicken Bone*	D	59
I do not know / Whether I have the	*Surprise*	I	145
I dreamt I had a tiny ear growing inside my	*Future Nightmare*	*	55
I felt myself falling through a hole in the	*Return*	D	189
I have forgotten it, / The guilt which lay	*The Losing*	D	104
I have known you in another life	*Shadows*	I	89
I have nothing, / Unless I have all	*Spur*	D	163
I have peeled off the façade	*Onion*	D	93
I have scrubbed the house from top to	*Disillusionment*	D	88
I have wilfully flicked an ounce of flesh	*Rejection*	D	51
I hear an inner thump and must express	*Individuation*	D	156
I hear time's whispering silence in my ears	*Time's Whispering*	*	71
I hung upon the splintering beam of oak	*Fire Song*	*	69
I know a man / Who goes to church	*Crocodile*	*	72
I lay on the garden hammock / Stared up	*Conviction*	D	137
I sang a song of yearning and derision	*Corn Song*	D	214
I see you shadow-bound / Between the	*Shades*	*	49
I thought of you, picking grapes	*The Bore*	I	70
I thought she was so cool, so untouchable	*Trendy People*	I	138
I wish, I wait. I wait and I wish.	*Ballad*	D	73
I wonder what this constellation will be	*I Wonder What This*	D	190
I wrote away at ease until the poets	*Why Write?*	I	171
Id, / Evil id, / Burning cantankerous in	*Evil*	I	195
Ideas / Like ants / Multiply, swarm and	*Ants*	*	60
If I could sink down into my stomach	*Fulcrum*	D	106
If we never see each other again,	*Parting*	D	50
If you could love the person / Whom you	*Combat*	*	41
I'll give you a ningo pin, / A pin of God	*The Ningo Pin*	D	196
In a café by a window / There is no	*Vacuum*	I	72
In another life / Many transmigrations	*Lizard*	D	119
In Chawton House, the birthplace of	*Chawton House*	D	181
In France / The mistletoe sprouts on oak	*Parasite*	I	108

In me / You stay / White fire	*Through the Needle's*	*	22
In the antique shop on the corner	*Torpor*	I	53
In the falling away, / Grey wings of bird	*Sin*	D	80
In the peak of the rush-hour / The man	*Off Peak*	I	68
In the tube / At twenty minutes to nine	*Tube-Time*	I	32
In this Victorian parlour / Eggshell walls	*Interior*	I	143
Infection / Takes us out of the cardboard	*Infection*	I	221
Inside my head / Fly / A white bird and	*Song of the Crow*	I	235
Invisible strings / Sweep the squares	*Paper Children*	I	39
Is it a nightmare or a dream? / I see	*Dream of Oxford*	I	158
Is this an eternal waking / After the eye	*Afterwards*	D	184
It does not lie in a house and home	*Security*	D	210
'It is rude,' said Alice, 'to make personal	*Questions and*	I	188

K

Keats wrote somewhere / That when	*The Line of Memory*	I	200
Knowing how he does not love you	*Spiral of Light*	D	60

L

Leap into the white void of Monday	*Monday Morning*	I	29
Leaves crush branches, / Emerald sting	*Cycle*	I	240
Let the ugly speak / In angular smiles	*The Ugly*	D	97
Life is not symmetrical, / A layer of	*See-Saw*	D	105
Lilting and loving, loving and lilting	*The Ballroom*	D	38
Lime teeth, / Straw of grass	*Kibbutz*	I	71
Listening / To the hardy battleaxe	*War Baby*	I	230
Listening to two conversations at once	*Crossed Line*	I	46
Lost between stone basins / And lions	*Lost Between Stone*	I	102
Love, once wanted, / Panacea to blunt	*Double Edged*	*	30

M

May / Peace birds trees sway / Welcome	*It Will Pass*	*	64
Midnight at the station / Shadows	*Midnight at the*	I	152
Midnight in my square bedsitter	*Nocturne*	D	125
Morning wakening, / The chalk-white	*Wakening*	D	102
Mother breaks through / The barriers	*Time*	I	26
My heart like frozen seaweed hangs	*Love*	D	134

N

Nature often belies living experience	*Nature*	D	143
Net curtains quiver / Like loops of jelly	*Two o'clock*	*	33
No better than the next / We rise and fall	*Routine*	I	134
No further can I go surely / Than to sink	*No Further Can I Go*	I	245
No moment will ever be more real than	*Through the Barrier*	I	38
No one / Can wipe out the fear that is	*Fear*	D	136
No one knows, / Where all the energy	*Preserve*	D	202
No security is possible, gateway to your	*Gift*	D	57
Not to see him again / Never the eyes	*Not to See Him*	*	58
Now / No love is here / To you / Rolled	*No Resting Place*	I	220
Now that the pendulum has swung	*Time Suspended*	D	108
Now that you are thirty / You have	*Photo*	I	218

O

Oh black and white machine of information	*Television*	I	166
On a primrose day in March	*Lemon*	I	111
On a windy morning in October	*Primary School*	*	46
On each shoulder is perched an object	*Duality*	D	75
On the corner of the arcade / Between	*Grief*	D	187
On the boat pub / Pretentious / Sea curls	*Night*	I	149
On this afternoon, / Tranquil gold	*Maternity*	D	146
One man was there / I loved / Face black	*Black and White U.*	*	43

One soul was lost. / It went tumbling	*Tunnel*	D	145
Only God knows the truth / Of the	*Knowledge*	D	209
Our friendship came to nothing, petered	*Burnt Out by ...*	D	63
Our love, fulfilled, would not be so	*Separation*	D	56
Out of the barren mind / Flew	*Wallflower*	I	246
Over the hills / Olive-black trees and	*Lost*	D	79
Over the morning / Hangs	*Portent*	I	51

P

Pain produces logic / To anaesthetise	*Roaming*	I	180
Parabola of water. / Hoop bent	*Water-Bird*	D	54
Party games are fun. / Let's throw away	*Party Games*	I	156
Pass on to the next / It grows	*Continue*	D	141
Pause, / While London changes	*Trafalgar*	I	73
Peach row of faces / Frozen into scrutiny	*Six Haikus*	I	226
People/Cluster like clover in the meadows	*Four-Leaved*	I	211
Perhaps this daily journal, / Pages of red	*The Search*	I	170
Pity / Passes through the layered	*Pity*	I	90
Please believe / That I want nothing	*Facets*	D	64
Potted plant between the lace of curtains	*Cactus*	I	121
Problems/That litter the mind like pebbles	*Success*	I	207

R

Rat-race, / Squeaks in the running	*Rat-Race*	I	203
Reality painful / As gasping fish out of	*Quick Birth*	D	25
Reality smiles, / Does not grow any	*Reality Smiles*	*	18
Red telephone kiosk / Leaning against	*Time Machine*	I	94
Respect for the elders, / Is it a tyranny	*Respect for the Elders*	I	227
Rosanna is silent and blonde and haughty	*Rosanna*	I	136
Rush-hour malaise. / Slow plodding of	*The Blind Man*	I	67

S

Sanity lies in emotional wholeness	*Sanity*	I	193
Satan grew so bright/That he sparked out	*God and Satan*	I	191
Saturday night / The broken down fire	*Saturday Night*	*	26
Save this soul / Catch its dropping	*Save This Soul*	D	195
Scorching light of day / White fire	*Morning*	I	28
Scrawny blue-veined hand still clutching	*Old Woman*	I	110
Sharpen the brain / To a fine point of	*Brain*	I	182
She laughed. 'I looked out of the window	*Twins*	D	162
She searched for happiness / As if it were	*She Searched for*	D	182
She slept in a chair by the table	*Dreams Talk*	*	28
She speaks glibly of intellectual despair	*Cynic*	*	44
She wants to be happy. / Her voice is	*Façade*	I	197
Silently, as the days pass, / We wait for	*Oyster*	I	208
Sitting at twin tables / I see	*Fishes*	I	60
Sleep in wonder. / Do not know where	*Interval*	D	130
Slowly the evil / Has seeped into my soul	*The Ten Days of*	I	177
Slowly the sweet-sour juice trickling	*Grape Picking*	D	34
Slowly / Unfolds / White salt peace	*Peace*	I	247
Smile upon us, lazy beauty, / Out of	*The Vision*	D	111
Smiled upon a face / That offered nothing	*Smiled upon a Face*	I	239
So I survived and compromised with	*Regeneration*	D	101
So many gaps, / White patches, which	*Percentage*	D	89
So many things given / Mornings that	*Deserted*	*	50
Some eagle hovers overhead	*Call*	I	25
Something / Of Hell / I saw / With this	*Foretaste*	I	137
Standing in the black rain	*Passing*	D	62
Stay attuned to the forces of life	*Pulse*	D	140
Strange to see this familiar face	*Dust*	I	42
Strength of you / Crag of shouldera	*Honesty*	*	23
Stretched out in a darkened room	*Vision*	D	103
Sun on the track / Three rods of fire	*Sun on the Track*	I	244

Sunday afternoon. / Out of the glass-	*Park-Time*	I	86
Sunday afternoon, / White as salt	*Salt*	*	52
Sunday television, an Italian wartime	*Reminder*	I	167
Sunflayed, / Cross-kneed upon steps	*On the Steps*	I	97

T

Take a petal, imprint it on your mind	*Meditation*	D	74
Taken by surprise / I squirm	*Food-Time*	I	118
Ten years ago they sat together at a	*The Wedding*	D	67
Tepid afternoon tea-leaf tea / Fills	*Stifled*	I	82
The birds wing jerkily across the mauve	*Flight*	I	125
The black days, / Metallic white sky	*The Waiting*	D	116
The boast / Spilled out of my lips	*The Boast*	I	59
The book of my mind lies open	*Schizophrenia*	D	84
The broken-down fire / Fuses the flat	*Ago*	D	144
The bus is swamped with raincoats	*Bus*	I	115
The cat, a seething kettle, / Paws and	*Aversion*	I	31
The challenge of an enemy	*The Enemy*	I	75
The coach is flashing through the hills	*Misunderstanding*	I	88
The consolation of illusion / Love and	*Consolation of I.*	*	36
The crazy sect are dancing / Along	*Street Dance*	I	81
The criminal is ill, / Steals in surprise	*Topsy-Turvy*	*	32
The daddy long legs / Cannot scuttle	*Insect*	I	165
The day I put away the tranquillisers	*Awakening*	D	171
The day slips across the murmuring sea	*Day and Night*	*	68
The death of someone you love	*Inconsolation*	D	197
The earth turns rebel against itself	*Day*	I	23
The empty spaces and wasted days	*Resurgence*	D	192
The essence of goodness / However	*The Will*	I	189
The falling in love down through a hole	*Falling*	D	39
The fat shopper in the fitting-room	*Outsize*	I	74
The first time I glimpsed Hell	*Preview*	D	29

The girl in purple trousers lay on the	*Release*	D	149
The girl sways her pregnant hips	*Earthquake*	*	56
The girl with the operated nose	*Change*	D	91
The God in my head is more real	*Skull-Light*	D	127
The green eyes of the black tomcat	*Jealousy*	I	183
The half people / Who live cramped days	*Frost*	I	224
The human soul floats down from	*The Soul*	D	198
The laughter grew / Into gold coils	*The Laughter*	D	52
The Man on the Cross, He rose	*Question*	D	158
The mouse / A tiny grey ball of fur	*Mouse*	I	164
The park on Easter Monday	*Bank Holiday*	I	85
The party was a slit of light under the door	*Party Time*	I	155
The person who knows you well	*Display*	I	187
The pigeon coos mercilessly / Outside	*Intercom*	I	37
The poet looks out / Of his head / Sieves	*The Poet*	I	172
The pounding Beethoven, / Beats	*The Deaf Ear*	I	169
The railway line of life / Never to be	*To Forestall*	I	112
The silence has been broken / By a string	*The Evening Class*	I	133
The smile, / A long-remembered habit	*The Smile*	I	209
The snow is falling February white	*Hospital in Winter*	D	86
The soul searcher / Lays aside his pen	*Conflict*	D	165
The spirit entered them; / Salt smoking	*Insight*	D	200
The Stoic / Thickens his skin with oil	*Two Cures*	I	212
The telephone / Black furry ear	*Telephone*	I	45
The torn fingernail, which you will pull	*Nail Armour*	D	115
The Tube on a Saturday evening	*Tube*	I	131
The washing-machine's stomach	*Launderette*	I	43
The wasted years / Thrown down a well	*Wasted Years*	I	222
The waves roll in / Day after day	*Waves*	D	199
The will frittered out / Would not obey	*Will*	*	37
There are signs, / Strange to interpret	*Signs*	D	203
There is a gold door in the sky	*Gold Door*	D	193
There is a madwoman gaunt and brown	*The Madwoman*	D	95

There is a test-card C of selfhood	*Keyboard*	D	107
'There is an answer to every problem	*Holocaust*	D	164
There is no cure for being one person	*Selfhood*	D	128
There was the first man / And the first	*Fallen Away*	I	234
They are mocking the devils within me	*Doubt*	D	167
They cut a slice out of the brain,	*Leucotomy*	D	85
They didn't mean to quarrel.	*The Quarrel*	D	48
They scrub the drawers / And sweep	*Housewarming*	*	62
They spoke blunt friendship / And their	*Widow Spider*	I	216
Things are not so easy for you now, my love	*Before and After*	*	54
Thinking is away from the grain	*Blue*	*	29
Thirst. / A crystal glass ball of ice-cold	*Water*	D	172
This death / I cannot quite believe in	*Shock*	D	185
This dismembered leg / From an ancient	*Age*	I	103
This hypnotist / Has a sandalwood voice	*Spellbound*	D	40
This park greenery / Overwhelms	*Fear of the Lone Self*	*	75
This passage along the days, / Does it	*Evolution*	D	205
This restaurant is like a fore-echo	*The Waiter*	I	119
Three words. / Brief answer to his	*Incommunicado*	I	52
Through a forest of taboos and ill-fortune	*Needlepoint*	I	210
Through bleary lattice-work of rain	*Rainy Day in the*	I	87
Through the railings, / Beyond the rail-	*Platform*	I	153
Thursday afternoons are for double	*Double Biology*	I	109
Tightening threads break through	*Over-Exposure*	I	201
Time frozen into ice-drops / Clings	*Time Frozen*	*	70
Tired of pure thoughts, crisp, snowflake	*Current of Belief*	I	198
To be loved / Is to stop thinking	*Protection*	D	41
To hear sometimes the grey groan of	*Tryptich*	D	157
To pay back in energy / The gift I have	*The Talents*	D	150
To run into a long tunnel, blackness	*Poetry*	D	126
To wake up from a three o'clock	*Nightmare*	D	121
Today, / Floating on an eiderdown of	*Feathers*	D	120
Try to absorb / The news on television	*Passive Involvement*	I	168

Twin pawns of ivory on a chessboard	*Duel*	D	161
Two decades and a half have passed	*Creation*	D	135

U

Uncorrupted, He participated, / Tore off	*Reconciliation*	D	207
Unlike the gypsy in the tent with a glass	*The Future*	I	194
Untidy Friday afternoons, / Ends of	*Friday Afternoons*	I	83

V

Virginia saw it too, / The door	*Neurasthenia*	D	83

W

Walking away from the doctor's	*Malaise*	I	106
Walking between the great stone	*Image*	I	132
Walking one by one / Down the white	*Lunchtime*	I	63
Walking over the grass on an evening in	*Label*	I	129
Walking, windswept / Over the slatted	*Pier*	I	123
Wallflowers scorching blood in July	*Summer*	I	61
Wandering through the days	*Wandering ...*	D	61
Warm, friendly voice, / Cultivated	*Sophistication*	I	217
We follow our gods / Doggedly	*We Follow Our Gods*	I	236
We lay in a circle on the carpet, heads	*Hypnosis*	I	139
We live in the age of psychology	*Psychology*	I	192
We met on a blistering summer's	*Ugliness*	I	58
We sat in the damp evening air	*Confession*	D	47
We were talking in a hut on a strange	*The Bluffer*	I	49
Weep before God / When the ice breaks	*Weep Before God*	D	174
Whale ideas / Blubber home	*Whale Ideas*	*	19
What is the use of this strained sensibility	*Song of a...*	D	112
When all the love has dwindled away	*Acorn*	I	113

When his arms closed around you	When His Arms...	D	43
When I tore away the curtain of my	Revelation	D	81
When I was a child, a naughty child	Nice Child	D	27
When I was fifteen, / I stood in front of	Devils	D	160
When I was young and the rain poured	Worms	I	50
When it is cold and empty, / Black sky	Belief	D	204
When morning is whiter than shell	When Morning Is	I	30
When my anger broods and stirs	Three Witches	*	48
When the dog ran away in the middle of	Loss	I	150
When the door opens, / The silence will	When the Door	D	194
When the pain comes / Gold spots upon	The Fainting	I	154
When the pain rings true, / Like charnel	Instant	I	190
When we met, / Cardboard figures	Cut-outs	D	53
When you love someone so strangely	When You Love...	D	42
Where the will lies / Flicker to the right	Decision	D	151
White dots in the air / That fizzle	Silence	D	177
Who loves the grey tent of darkness	Winter	I	151
'Why do you smile all the time'	Smile	D	44
Why, when I look at silver, / Can I not see	Silver	*	74
Will eat / Only the bitter flesh of apple	Ascetic, The	I	229
Winter dampness is a fungus	Winter Dampness	*	17
Wish to be reclaimed by the Spirit	Reclamation	D	166
Without the selectivity / Of a brain filter	Filter	I	181

Y

Yoga dance, / Fly away to the north and	Yoga Dance	D	110
You are a non-person. / You do not have	Reflector	I	204
You are a spider flashing out silks,	Spider	D	129
You can try / For a minute, for an hour	The Aim	D	65
You hate my barren mind / And long for	Camera	I	232
You have chosen the hard road	The Hard Road	D	23
You know I feel for you, / Your every	Clam	D	58